A Message from the Scotch Beef Club...

Warm hospitality, fantastic scenery, and fine food, are all contributory factors to a superb 'Scottish Experience'.

The Scots' longheld reputation for hospitality has, I suspect, been gained from centuries of tradition - travellers in bygone days expected always to find food and shelter in the homes of their kinsfolk, or even of mere acquaintances. A letter of introduction sufficed to open the door of cottage or castle.

**Brian M. Simpson
Chief Executive**

The fine foods of Scotland and the varied landscape are inter-linked - because Scotland's rich diversity of terrain provides the most natural environment for all the fish, game birds, venison, lamb and beef for which this small country is internationally renowned. With regard to the latter meats, it is pleasing to me to see so many Scotch Beef Club restaurants - a European group which sprang directly from the international reputation for the quality of our beef. Members are ranged across Europe, from the Isle of Skye right down to Sicily, and many of the Scottish establishments are featured in this year's Stevensons Guide.

Here in Scotland today's traveller still seeks comfort, traditional hospitality and the ultimate eating experience. A letter of introduction is no longer the only way to open the door to Scottish hospitality - all the hotels in this book have been personally selected by Alan Stevenson, to help our discerning visitors access that same warm welcome and achieve 1990's 'customer satisfaction.'

STEVENSONS
SCOTLAND'S GOOD HOTEL BOOK
1997

Published by: Alan Stevenson Publications
4/3 Boat Green
Canonmills
EDINBURGH
EH3 5LL
Tel: 0131-556 2200
Fax: 0131-557 6324

Copyright © 1996 Stevensons - Scotland's Good Hotel Book - Second Edition

North American Representative: M & M Travel, Inc.
4425 Randolph Road
Suite 315, Charlotte
N.C. 28211
Tel: (704) 365 6500
1-800-365-6537
Fax: (704) 365 3800

ISBN 0 9526595 1 4

Price: £4.95
$10.00 from USA agent only. (Includes Canada)

Map by: Baynefield Carto-Graphics Ltd.
Printed in Scotland by: Macdonald Lindsay Pindar plc
Front Cover: Stonefield Castle Hotel, Argyll.

STEVENSONS

SCOTLAND'S GOOD HOTEL BOOK

1997

The breathtaking natural beauty of Scotland has captivated poets, inspired artists and seduced travel writers from around the world.

Its charm is blended from the craggy mountains, unspoilt glens, serene lochs and magnificent coastline to provide a landscape unique to our shores.

Complementing the outstanding quality of these natural assets is the warmth and friendliness of welcome, the excellence of service and the fine cuisine visitors can be assured of from this personal selection of fine hotels.

Publisher, Alan Stevenson, has travelled the length and breadth of Scotland to make his unique choice of distinguished destinations offering the best in

Alistair Campbell
Managing Director of Stonefield Castle Group

Scottish hospitality. As Managing Director of a small group of privately owned, and distinctly different, Scottish hotels, I am delighted he has again singled out Stonefield as one of his favourites.

Scotland has so much to offer and is unashamedly scenic in any season. It is impossible to put into words the beauty of a summer sunset over a highland loch; the changing hue of the autumn countryside; the stillness of a crisp winter morning or the joy of a fresh spring day.

These pleasures must be experienced - a warm welcome awaits.

Alistair Campbell

A Selection of Scottish Jewellery

Large Silver Plaid Brooch with real Stone.

£190.00

The Luckenbooth brooch - a design of great antiquity from the "Locked Booths" around St Giles in Edinburgh.

Available in Silver or Gold
with Amethyst or Golden Citrine Stone from

£60.00

Quaichs (not illustrated).

Available in pewter, silver plate
and sterling silver. Prices (pewter) from

£16.00

R. L. CHRISTIE
WATCHMAKERS & JEWELLERS

17 - 20 BANK STREET EDINBURGH EH1 2LN
Tel 0131 225 8114   Fax 0131 225 5436

Tel/code No from USA/Canada 01144-131 225 8114

Major credit cards accepted Insurance and postage not included

STEVENSONS

SCOTLAND'S GOOD HOTEL BOOK

1997

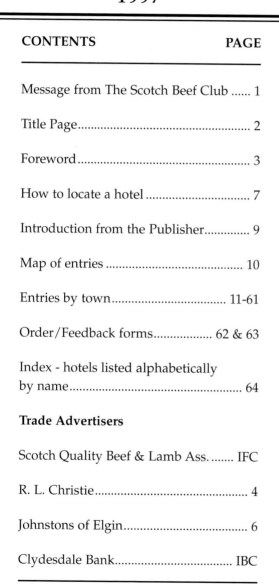

CONTENTS   PAGE

STEVENSONS
SCOTLAND'S GOOD HOTEL BOOK
1997

1. First look at the map of **Scotland** at the beginning of the publication, on page 10. The place name of the hotels I am featuring will be highlighted in bold type.

2. Once you have pinpointed your location follow along the top of the pages, which are arranged alphabetically, until you arrive at your location.

3. If you already have the name of the hotel and wish to know if it is included, turn to the index at the back of the book. Hotels are listed alphabetically.

4. In some cases where hotels are located close to major towns, they may be shown under that town with the exact location in brackets. For example, INVERNESS (Culloden), ST. ANDREWS (Lundin Links).

5. **Price guide:** This quote is based on an overnight stay single & double. Normally this is for bed & breakfast but sometimes if dinner is included it will be indicated. (includes dinner).

Letham Grange

6. The above prices are quoted for a one night stay, but most of the establishments in this book offer reductions for stays of two or more nights. Also please enquire about seasonal bargain 'breaks'.

7. **Black Bull Logo:** Any establishment which displays "The Black Bull Logo" is a member of the Scotch Beef Club. This club is unashamedly based on quality. Only those serving specially selected Scotch Beef to a very high standard are admitted as members.

Photo by
David C Crawford

Loch an Eilein,
Near Aviemore,
Inverness-shire.

STEVENSONS

SCOTLAND'S GOOD HOTEL BOOK

1997

A Message from the Publisher...

Welcome to the second edition of **Stevensons - Scotland's Good Hotel Book 1997**. The photograph on the page opposite expresses more than I can put into words about our beautiful country - it is quite unique. The reaction from hoteliers and the response from readers to the first edition in 1996 was overwhelming and beyond all expectation. Regular users of STEVENSONS will not only find old favourites, but I have included many more establishments to replace those which for one reason or another have been deleted. A further development for 1997 is the appointment of M & M Travel Inc., in Charlotte, North Carolina as official agents for STEVENSONS in the USA. Managing Director Cate Murrell will undertake bookings direct with hotels. Full details of M & M Travel Inc., can be located on the title page.

Alan Stevenson
Publisher

This book is a personal selection of establishments and reflects everything which is good in Scottish hospitality. All maintain and sustain high standards and a warm welcome is assured. The popularity of the first edition was in part due to SCOTLAND having its own Good Hotel Book and not being consigned as part of another hotel guide. Plans are well under way for the third edition in 1998 and again I am indebted to the advice and support which I have received from all hoteliers.

A special mention to the Scotch Quality Beef & Lamb Association for their continued support in what has been a very difficult year for them. Enjoy your copy of **Stevensons - 1997** and I look forward to 1998 with great confidence.

Photo by
Yerbury of Edinburgh

INTRODUCTION

ARDOE HOUSE HOTEL

Ardoe House Hotel, Blairs, South Deeside Road, Aberdeen AB12 5YP
Tel: 01224 867355 Fax: 01224 861283 USA Toll Free Tel: 1-800-365-6537

Enclosed by trees and rich foliage Ardoe House stands on high ground commanding a magnificent view of the river Dee and open country. This baronial mansion was built in 1878 in the style favoured by Queen Victoria with lofty turrets, towers and spires. Today and after extensive renovation the hotel offers its guests every modern comfort, yet retaining the style and charm of a country mansion. The wood panelled dining room is within the original house. Menus are imaginative and varied and give great attention to the flavour and presentation of the best of local produce. Whatever your taste in cuisine the array of delights available will more than match your expectations. Treat yourself by checking into a different room each time – every room in the old house is exclusive and has its own unique atmosphere. The dining capacity of 200 and the ability to accommodate 300 people theatre style makes this hotel one of the most sought after venues in the area.

Open: *All year*
No. Rooms: *71 En Suite 71*
Room telephones: *Yes*
TV in Rooms: *Yes*
Pets: *Yes*   **Children:** *Yes*
Disabled: *Yes*

Swimming Pool/Health Club: *No*
Conference Facilities: *4 venues from 2-200*
Price Guide: *Single £62.50-£123.00 Double £92.00-£150.00*
Location: *B9077, 3 miles west of Aberdeen.*

MARYCULTER HOUSE HOTEL

Maryculter, South Deeside Road, Aberdeen AB12 5GB
Tel: 01224 732124 Fax: 01224 733510 USA Toll Free Tel: 1-800-365-6537

Maryculter House Hotel stands in 5 acres of woodland and landscaped gardens on the south bank of the river Dee. The house originates from 1255 when it was built as a preceptory by Walter Bisset a member of a powerful Anglo-Norman family. The gardens are a feature of this hotel as are the 23 bedrooms individually furnished and decorated in a style in keeping with this historic and elegant building. The "Poachers Bar" enjoys breathtaking views over the river Dee where one can dine informally or The Priory Room provides a splendid setting for a candlelit dinner which includes a varied menu of Scottish dishes with light French delicacies. For conferences and banquets the Templar Suite can accommodate up to 200 with its own entrance and car parking. There are further facilities for smaller meetings and private dinner parties. Only 8 miles from Aberdeen there are 3 golf courses within the immediate area - shooting, fishing and other leisure pursuits can be arranged. Step back in time to the days of lairds, castles and clans, and experience first hand the lifestyle of Scottish nobility.

Open: *All year*	**Swimming Pool/Health Club:** *No*
No. Rooms: *23 En Suite 23*	**Conference Facilities:** *Up to 200*
Room telephones: *Yes*	**Price Guide:** *Single from £65.00 Double/Twin from £85.00*
TV in Rooms: *Yes*	**Location:** *B9077 Banchory-Aberdeen (South Deeside Road) 5 miles from Aberdeen, 1 mile west of B979 & B9077 junction. Signposted.*
Pets: *By arrangement*	
Children: *Yes*	
Disabled: *Yes*	

SKENE HOUSE HOLBURN

Union Grove, Aberdeen AB10 6SY
Tel: 01224 580000 Fax: 01224 585193 USA Toll Free Tel: 1-800-365-6537

"A home away from home" is the only way to describe this new venture in Aberdeen. Although an American concept it is "catching on" in this country not only for the business person but the annual holiday which most of us take. This project is an extension to Skene House at Rosemount Viaduct in the same city and offers luxury accommodation on a grand scale. 1, 2 or 3 bedroomed suites with kitchen and lounge are your choices. Interior designers have created outstandingly attractive luxury suites from traditional to contemporary, blending furniture, fabrics, prints and colours. Although situated near the intersection of Union Street & Holburn Street provision has been made for ample private car parking so it is only a minutes walk to enjoy the city of Aberdeen, the Granite City, where there is much to do and see. Restaurants abound, shopping centres, art galleries, Her Majesty's Theatre etc. Add the maid service and complimentary continental breakfast and there is no better value around, whether you stay 1 night, a week, a month, or a year.

Open: *All year*	**Swimming Pool/Health Club:** *Sauna/Steam Room*
No. Rooms: *35 En Suite 35*	**Conference Facilities:** *Up to 12 director level*
Room telephones: *Yes*	**Price Guide:** *1 Bedroom suite £82.00 2Bedroom suite £99.00*
TV in Rooms: *Yes*	*- £119.00*
Pets: *By arrangement*	**Location:** *Corner of Holburn Street/Union Grove*
Children: *Yes*	
Disabled: *Unsuitable*	

THAINSTONE HOUSE HOTEL & COUNTRY CLUB

Inverurie, Aberdeenshire AB51 5NT
Tel: 01467 621643 Fax: 01467 625084 USA Toll Free Tel: 1-800-365-6537

Classical elegance blends with contemporary excellence at Thainstone House. Set in 40 acres the hotel provides everything that is luxurious offering a range of leisure activities including a Roman style indoor pool, gymnasium and jacuzzi. There is a grand portal entrance, galleried reception area and Georgian restaurant. In the Simpson restaurant both a la carte and table d'hote menus are available offering a very good blend of different choices and drawing on the local resources for which the farmland around Thainstone is renowned. Over the years the bedroom capacity has been increased to 48, all en suite, and with every facility. Great care and planning reflects the high quality of accommodation and host Jane Robertson and her staff immediately put guests at ease in this warm, relaxing hotel. Thainstone makes an ideal base for touring the area and is in the heart of the whisky, castle and fishing trail.

Open: *All year*	**Disabled:** *Yes*
No. Rooms: *48 En Suite 48*	**Swimming Pool/Health Club:** *Yes*
Room telephones: *Yes*	**Conference Facilities:** *Theatre – up to 400*
TV in Rooms: *Yes*	**Price Guide:** *Single from £65.00 Double from £78.00*
Pets: *No dogs*	**Location:** *Off A96 south of Inverurie.*
Children: *Yes*	

THE GEAN HOUSE

Gean Park, Tullibody Road, Alloa, Clackmannanshire FK10 2HS
Tel: 01259 219275 Fax: 01259 213827 USA Toll Free Tel: 1-800-365-6537

The Gean (the Scots word for a wild cherry tree, and refers to the number of these which surround it) is an imposing mansion set in wooded parkland with attractive views across the Ochil Hills. Elegance, grandeur and intimacy are all words that describe The Gean House owned and run by Sandra Frost who takes a very active role in maintaining the high standards accorded an STB 4 Crown De Luxe rating. The bedrooms are a delight - very spacious and richly decorated with every facility - the public rooms are a joy to behold with fresh flowers and inglenook fireplaces. Drawing from the best home grown produce and game available the chef creates dishes recognised by "The Taste of Scotland" which are complemented by a carefully chosen wine list. Both Table d'hote and a la carte menus are available. The Gean House is situated in country familiar to Scottish heroes such as William Wallace and Rob Roy and in addition there are many historical sites to visit including Stirling Castle. This small luxury hotel offers every comfort in a setting of complete tranquility.

Open: *All year*	**Swimming Pool/Health Club:** *No*
No. Rooms: *7 En Suite 7*	**Conference Facilities:** *Up to 50*
Room telephones: *Yes*	**Price Guide:** *Single £80.00 Double £120.00-£140.00*
TV in Rooms: *Yes*	**Location:** *A907 from Kincardine Bridge or Stirling.*
Pets: *No* **Children:** *Yes*	*Entrance on B9096 Tullibody Road less than 5*
Disabled: *Yes*	*mins. from Alloa Town Hall roundabout.*

LETHAM GRANGE RESORT

Colliston, By Arbroath, Angus DD11 4RL

Tel: 01241 890373 Fax: 01241 890414 USA Toll Free Tel: 1-800-365-6537

This Victorian mansion has been beautifully renovated to reflect the era of an earlier age complete with period paintings, original ceilings, fireplaces and staircases. This luxurious hotel and its setting is complemented by 2 golf courses and a curling rink for those so inclined. In addition to the spacious well decorated bedrooms which are in keeping with the grand style of building there are now a further 22 bedrooms only 300 yards from the main building. All bedrooms are en suite and have every modern convenience. Golfers can relax in the large Sweep 'n' Swing lounge or enjoy the best of Scottish or International cuisine in the Rosehaugh restaurant. Host Alan Wright has a 'hands on approach' which gives one a feeling of efficiency and good service - an aura of contentment exudes through the whole establishment. It is difficult to find a place of this calibre in this part of Scotland and it is ideally placed for visiting National Trust properties and Glamis Castle where the Queen Mother was born.

Open: *All year*
No. Rooms: *42 En Suite 42*
Room telephones: *Yes*
TV in Rooms: *Yes*
Pets: *By arrangement*
Children: *Yes*

Disabled: *Yes*
Swimming Pool/Health Club: *No*
Conference Facilities: *Up to 500*
Price Guide: *Single from £65.00   Double from £95.00*
Location: *From A92, Arbroath, take A933 to Colliston and turn right at sign to Letham Grange.*

THE ARDEONAIG HOTEL

South Loch Tayside, Perthshire FK21 8SU
Tel: 01567 820400 Fax: 01567 820282 USA Toll Free Tel: 1-800-365-6537

The Ardeonaig Hotel is situated on the south side of Loch Tay midway between Killin and Kenmore. The hotel, with Ben Lawers as a backdrop, is set in very attractive grounds overlooking Loch Tay and the hills beyond. Resident proprietors Alan and Eileen Malone have gone to extraordinary lengths to refurbish this hotel and always extend a very warm welcome to visitors where comfort and food are a premium. There are further plans to improve the building with a secluded courtyard for functional purposes as the scene lends itself to weddings on a smaller scale. There are 15 en suite and very comfortable bedrooms and Eileen has built up an enviable reputation for food. Her menus are a delight using only the best of produce which is in season – good honest Scottish traditional cooking at its best. This is an anglers paradise with the hotel owning salmon fishing rights on Loch Tay as well as fishing for trout and char. The hotel has its own harbour, boats, outboards, rod room and drying room. There are several golf courses within 25 minutes drive. Member of The Scotch Beef Club.

Open: *All year (Nov.-Mar. Limited Service)*	**Disabled:** *Limited*
No. Rooms: *15 En Suite 15*	**Swimming Pool/Health Club:** *No*
Room telephones: *No*	**Conference Facilities:** *Maximum 15*
TV in Rooms: *No*	**Price Guide:** *Single £66.00 (incl Dinner) Double £123.50 (incl. Dinner)*
Pets: *Yes* **Children:** *Yes*	**Location:** *7 miles from Killin on south bank of Loch Tay.*

BALCARY BAY HOTEL

Auchencairn, Near Castle Douglas, Kirkcudbrightshire DG7 1QZ
Tel: 01556 640217 Fax: 01556 640272 USA Toll Free Tel: 1-800-365-6537

Dating back to 1625 this splendid country house hotel stands in over 3 acres of grounds in a secluded situation on the shores of the bay. The hotel has commanding views of the Solway Coast and the Cumbrian Mountains. Owned and operated by the Lamb family, Balcary has a fascinating history with smugglers of a bygone era and the building retains much of the old character. Over the years the Lamb family have refurbished the hotel to reflect a high quality of accommodation and cuisine. The dining room provides high quality food using produce from the area. Galloway beef, lamb, lobster and Balcary Bay salmon are popular choices. The hospitality together with good food makes this the ideal holiday hotel to 'get away from it all'.

Open: *Early Mar.-mid Nov.*	**Swimming Pool/Health Club:** *No*
No. Rooms: *17 En Suite 17*	**Conference Facilities:** *No*
Room telephones: *Yes*	**Price Guide:** *Single £52.00 Double £94.00-£104.00*
TV in Rooms: *Yes*	**Location:** *A711 Dalbeattie-Kirkcudbright to Auchencairn.*
Pets: *Yes* **Children:** *Yes*	
Disabled: *Unsuitable*	

 AA ⊛

THE CAIRN LODGE

Orchil Road, Auchterarder, Perthshire PH3 1LX

Tel: 01764 662634 Fax: 01764 664866 USA Toll Free Tel: 1-800-365-6537

Recently extended and upgraded The Cairn Lodge is pleasantly situated in attractive gardens just outside this famous Perthshire village. Recently the Cairn Lodge has been awarded a STB rating of 4 crown de luxe and an AA food rosette. Famous for golf and Gleneagles just 'up the road'. Alex and Michelle McDonald – owners of The Cairn Lodge have transformed the hotel into one of the most popular venues in the area. The 7 en suite bedrooms are beautifully furnished to a high standard and equipped with every modern convenience. The Capercaille restaurant is renowned for its classical Scottish cuisine but also offers a wide range of dishes which are imaginatively prepared. There are spacious public rooms and the new extension at the rear of the hotel fits in perfectly with the original building. There are numerous leisure activities on offer. Apart from the world famous Gleneagles courses golfers are in easy reach of Carnoustie and St. Andrews. Whether its the swift, yet unobtrusive service, or the superior quality of the cuisine, The Cairn Lodge not only reaches the high standards its name suggests but, indeed, surpasses them.

Open: *All year*	**Swimming Pool/Health Club:** *No*
No. Rooms: *7 En Suite 7*	**Conference Facilities:** *Up to 25*
Room telephones: *Yes*	**Price Guide:** *Single from £55.00 Double from £80.00.*
TV in Rooms: *Yes*	**Location:** *Next to Gleneagles.*
Pets: *No* **Children:** *Yes*	
Disabled: *Unsuitable*	

CORROUR HOUSE HOTEL

Inverdruie, Aviemore PH22 1QH
Tel: 01479 810220 Fax: 01479 811500 USA Toll Free Tel: 1-800-365-6537

There are many hotels in Aviemore but my own choice would certainly be Corrour House Hotel which nestles 'off the beaten track' at Inverdruie just outside Aviemore on the south side of the village. A private and family run hotel this Victorian house stands in 4 acres of garden and woodland where deer and squirrels are regular visitors. Its isolation is to its advantage and there are fine views over Rothiemurchas Forest, the Lairig Ghru and the Cairngorm mountains. There is true highland hospitality here and hosts David & Sheana Catto cater entirely for their guests ensuring personal service but retaining an informal approach which makes one feel very comfortable. All seven bedrooms have been furnished to offer every modern comfort with en suite facilities and the drawing room with cosy fire offers one the feeling of contentment with a small refreshment before dinner. I can personally vouch for the cuisine - the menu changes on a daily basis with emphasis on fresh produce featuring prime Scottish beef, local game & venison, salmon & trout. An ideal base for touring the highlands of Scotland.

Open: *Feb.-Oct.*	**Swimming Pool/Health Club:** *No*
No. Rooms: *7 En Suite 7*	**Conference Facilities:** *No*
Room telephones: *Yes*	**Price Guide:** *B & B £34.00 Dinner B & B £54.00*
TV in Rooms: *Yes* **Pets:** *By arrange.*	*Weekly £325.00 Per Person, inc. VAT.*
Children: *Yes*	**Location:** *From south turn right at B970 before entering Aviemore. Clearly*
Disabled: *Unsuitable*	*signposted about ½ mile on B970 which leads to Coylumbridge.*

DARROCH LEARG HOTEL

Braemar Road, Ballater, Royal Deeside, Aberdeenshire AB35 5UX
Tel: 013397 55443 Fax: 013397 55252 USA Toll Free Tel: 1-800-365-6537

Darroch Learg stands in 5 acre grounds in a commanding position close to the charming tourist town of Ballater. The hotel boasts stunning views south across Royal Deeside. The calm and elegance of the former private residence have been retained by the present owners, Fiona and Nigel Franks. A very friendly and relaxed atmosphere prevails throughout the hotel with its elegant public rooms and very comfortable bedrooms. In addition to the 13 bedrooms in the main house there are five in Oakhall, a Scottish baronial house sharing the same grounds. Dinner is served in the conservatory with its wonderful outlook to the hills. Darroch Learg has been awarded 2 AA rosettes for the food which uses the best of Aberdeenshire's produce, including Aberdeen Angus beef, lamb, and fish. Ballater is a short distance from Balmoral and in an area renowned for its outstanding scenery, fine walks, outdoor sports and places of interest. The popular castle, and whisky trails are nearby.

Open: *All year except January*	**Swimming Pool/Health Club:** *No*
No. Rooms: *18 En Suite*	**Conference Facilities:** *Up to 20*
Room telephones: *Yes*	**Price Guide:** *Single £45.00 Double £35.00 - £55.00*
TV in Rooms: *Yes*	**Location:** *On A93 at the western end of Ballater on road to*
Pets: *Yes* **Children:** *Yes*	*Braemar.*
Disabled: *Yes*	

BANCHORY LODGE HOTEL

Banchory, Kincardineshire AB31 3HS
Tel: 01330 822625 Fax: 01330 825019 USA Toll Free Tel: 1-800-365-6537

This Deeside hotel which was formerly a 16th century coaching inn is spectacularly situated on the banks of the river Dee. The gardens reflect the care and attention taken by resident proprietor Margaret Jaffray with sweeping lawns down to the river bank and an abundance of flowers (especially the daffodils in spring). This care and attention continues its theme within the hotel where all the best qualities can be savoured. The bedrooms are very spacious and comfortable – designed with considerable flair and imagination. Many have views over the river. The dining room is a masterpiece. Popular menu items are of course Dee salmon and Aberdeen Angus beef but there are many alternatives served in the best traditions which have been painstakingly prepared. With family support from her son Duncan, Margaret creates an atmosphere of perfect tranquillity and if you want to escape the pressures of life Banchory Lodge is like 'a home from home'.

Open: *All year*	**Swimming Pool/Health Club:** *Sauna only*
No. Rooms: *22 En Suite 22*	**Conference Facilities:** *Up to 25*
Room telephones: *Yes*	**Price Guide:** *Single £72.00 Double £85.00-£135.00*
TV in Rooms: *Yes*	**Location:** *A93 North Deeside road from Aberdeen. Turn*
Pets: *Yes* **Children:** *Yes*	*down Dee Street from Main Street – 400 yards –*
Disabled: *No*	*hotel on your left.*

AUCHEN CASTLE

Beattock, By Moffat, Dumfriesshire DG10 9SH
Tel: 01683 300407 Fax: 01683 300667 USA Toll Free Tel: 1-800-365-6537

This impressive baronial mansion is located almost halfway between Carlisle and Edinburgh or Glasgow just off the A74/M74 but isolated from the main traffic. It stands in 50 acres of trees and fine shrubs and was originally the home of the William Younger family (well known Scottish brewers). Many of the original features have been retained and it is very comfortably furnished and decorated throughout. 10 of the 25 en suite bedrooms are in a modern wing – accommodation of a high standard with all modern conveniences. Combined with good home cooking with many variations Auchen Castle is the ideal place for a stopover whether travelling North or South. The countryside of Burns, Scott and Buchan the area entices you to remain longer than planned and owner Mrs Hazel Beckh makes that little bit of an extra effort to welcome guests – whether returning or visiting for the first time.

Open: *All year except 3 weeks over Christmas & New Year*	**Disabled:** *Unsuitable*
No. Rooms: *25 En Suite 25*	**Swimming Pool/Health Club:** *No*
Room telephones: *Yes*	**Conference Facilities:** *Small business meetings up to 30*
TV in Rooms: *Yes*	**Price Guide:** *Single £51.50 Double £60.00-£80.00*
Pets: *Yes* **Children:** *Yes*	**Location:** *Access direct from A74/M74 one mile North of Beattock Village.*

PITTODRIE HOUSE

Chapel of Garioch, Near. Pitcaple, Aberdeenshire AB51 5HS
Tel: 01467 681444 Fax: 01467 681648 USA Toll Free Tel: 1-800-365-6537

Pittodrie House is an imposing turreted Scottish baronial style mansion dating back to 1480. It stands at the foot of Bennachie within a 3000 acre estate and the grounds around the building are something to behold. As one might expect the hotel is a popular venue for weddings. The ancestral home of Theo Smith the family paintings and antiques have been retained in all the reception rooms and bedrooms to keep the atmosphere of a country house rather than a hotel. You can make yourself at home in front of log fires and taste one of more than 90 malt whiskies stocked in the comfortable bar. All 27 bedrooms are furnished to a high standard, all are en suite and have all the features you would expect from a modern hotel. The orangery is an extension of the dining room where the menu is changed daily. Specialities are game, smoked and fresh fish and Aberdeen Angus beef. Vegetables and herbs are grown in the walled garden. There is a list of more than 200 wines which specialises in Clarets and new world wines. Pittodrie House is only 20 minutes from Aberdeen airport.

Open: *All year*	**Swimming Pool/Health Club:** *No*
No. Rooms: *27 En Suite 27*	**Conference Facilities:** *Yes*
Room telephones: *Yes*	**Price Guide:** *Single £120.00 Double £140.00*
TV in Rooms: *Yes*	**Location:** *Off A96 just north of Pitcaple. 20 miles north of*
Pets: *Yes* **Children:** *Yes*	*Aberdeen.*
Disabled: *Unsuitable*	

CONCHRA HOUSE HOTEL

Sallachy Road, Ardelve, Ross-shire IV40 8DZ

Tel: 01599 555233 Fax: 01599 555433 USA Toll Free Tel: 1-800-365-6537

This distinctive country house which dates back to the 1760s was originally the home of the local "Constable" responsible for affairs after the second Jacobite rising in 1745. Subsequently used as a hunting lodge the present owners Colin and Mary Deans have updated and refurbished the house into a very comfortable country house hotel. There are 6 conveniently sized bedrooms and because of their particular layout the twin second floor bedrooms make an excellent family suite offering that extra degree of privacy. Set in spacious grounds there is alternative accomodation in the form of farm cottages which are fully upgraded. Taste of Scotland members, the cuisine is excellent and includes dishes such as Mary's cream of celery soup, poached loch salmon and Victoria plum and almond flan. Conveniently placed for travel to the Isle of Skye and other destinations the accent at Conchra is on comfort and relaxation. Well recommended.

Open: *All year ex. Xmas/Hogm./New Yr.*	**Swimming Pool/Health Club:** *No*
No. Rooms: *6 En Suite 3*	**Conference Facilities:** *Yes*
Room telephones: *No*	**Price Guide:** *Single £40 B/B - £57 D.B.&B. Double £75 B/B*
TV in Rooms: *No*	*- £110 D.B.&B.*
Pets: *No* **Children:** *Yes*	**Location:** *From south continue westward on A87 past Dornie/Eilean Donan Castle.*
Disabled: *Unsuitable*	*Follow hotel signposts-turn right for ½ mile. (Sallachy/Killilan Road)*

COUL HOUSE HOTEL

Contin (By Strathpeffer), Ross-shire IV14 9EY
Tel: 01997 421487 Fax: 01997 421945 USA Toll Free Tel: 1-800-365-6537

Situated 17 miles west of Inverness Coul House Hotel was once the home of the ancient MacKenzies. For the past 19 years it has been the home of Martyn and Ann Hill who have maintained and sustained high standards. The house, which was originally built in 1821, has been extensively, though sympathetically, restored offering its guests a high standard of comfort whilst retaining all of the original character, charm and architecture. The bedroom capacity has been reduced by 1 this year to accommodate a luxurious bedroom with own lounge overlooking the magnificent views at the front of the hotel. The restaurant offers international cuisine skilfully blended with traditional Scottish fayre. The 20 fully equipped en suite bedrooms continue the elegant theme, all being individually designed by its owners. Most possess fine views of the forests and hills of the Strathconon valley. Although very popular with the fishing fraternity there are a number of leisure activities and local attractions include Loch Ness, Cawdor and the Culloden battle site of 1746.

Open: *All year*	**Swimming Pool/Health Club:** *No*
No. Rooms: *20 En Suite 20*	**Conference Facilities:** *Yes*
Room telephones: *Yes*	**Price Guide:** *Single £47.00-£60.50 Double £70.00-£97.00*
TV in Rooms: *Yes*	**Location:** *On A835 to Ullapool, 17 miles North West of*
Pets: *Yes* **Children:** *Yes*	*Inverness*
Disabled: *Yes*	

ALLT-CHAORAIN COUNTRY HOUSE

Crianlarich, Perthshire, FK20 8RU

Tel: 01838 300283 Fax: 01838 300238 USA Toll Free Tel: 1-800-365-6537

"In the middle of nowhere & in the middle of everywhere" is how resident proprietor Roger McDonald describes his country house. Allt-Chaorain is conveniently situated in an elevated position 500 yards from the roadside between Crianlarich and Tyndrum on the A82 and offers the perfect place to stop for a few days before travelling to the west and north west of Scotland. There are 7 comfortable bedrooms all with private facilities. A member of "Taste of Scotland" Allt-Chaorain is proud of their reputation for home cooked food which is made from local produce. The menu is changed daily. The wood panelled dining room caters for 6 persons to a table allowing the most reserved guests the chance of exchanging their days experiences. The hotel has a wonderful view over the Perthshire countryside and there is a very informal and friendly ambience at this establishment.

Open: *March - October*	**Swimming Pool/Health Club:** *No*
No. Rooms: *7 En Suite 7*	**Conference Facilities:** *No*
Room telephones: *Yes*	**Price Guide:** *Single £43-£49 Dinner £15-£18 Double £66-*
TV in Rooms: *Yes* **Pets:** *Yes*	*£78 Dinner £15-£18*
Children: *Over 7yrs*	**Location:** *Off A82 1 mile north of Crianlarich on*
Disabled: *Yes*	*Tyndrum Road.*

MURRAYPARK HOTEL
Connaught Terrace, Crieff, Perthshire PH7 3DJ
Tel: 01764 653731 Fax: 01764 655311 USA Toll Free Tel: 1-800-365-6537

This attractive hotel, operated by Ann and Noel Scott, is a large Victorian house set in the residential part of Crieff. Crieff is the 'gateway to the highlands' and is situated amongst some of the most scenic parts of Perthshire. The hotel enjoys a very high reputation in local parts – the restaurant is noted for its cuisine with menus based on good traditional Scottish food but with many interesting variations. The public rooms, dining room, bar and lounge are extremely comfortable with views looking out onto the well kept gardens. The 21 en suite bedrooms are tastefully decorated and equipped with every facility. The area is a golfers and anglers paradise. There are many other attractions to see and visit in the area including sites of special interest with Scotland's past. An ideal base for touring parts of the country.

Open: *All year*
No. Rooms: *20 En Suite 20*
Room telephones: *Yes*
TV in Rooms: *Yes*
Pets: *Yes* **Children:** *Yes*
Disabled: *Yes*

Swimming Pool/Health Club: *No*
Conference Facilities: *Up to 18*
Price Guide: *Single £52.00 Double £74.00*
Location: *Turn off A85 at Connaught Terrace, uphill to residential part of town.*

FERNIE CASTLE

Letham, by Cupar, Fife KY15 7RU
Tel: 01337 810381 Fax: 01337 810422 USA Toll Free Tel: 1-800-365-6537

Recently purchased by Marshall Stevens from the U.S.A. Fernie Castle Hotel dates from around 1353. This small individual castle is now a charming hotel with many unusual features including the circular tower, the ice house at the rear and the famous "Keep Bar" of a bygone era. Award winning chef Craig Millar prepares his dishes for the Auld Alliance Room in classical & French tradition using the best of local produce – fine crystal, fresh flowers adorn the dining room and candlelit dinners are a speciality. Bedrooms are well equipped (some with 4 posters) and offer every modern comfort. Within the wooded grounds reposes a small loch with swans and ducks where guests can stroll and admire the gentle Fife countryside. The 'home of golf' at St. Andrews is a mere 20 minutes drive from the hotel and in addition to other leisure activities there are places of interest to visit including National Trust For Scotland properties. I have known this establishment for many years now and feel a renewed confidence with the "hands on approach" of new owner Marshall Stevens.

Open: *All year*	**Disabled:** *Not suitable*
No. Rooms: *15 En Suite 15*	**Swimming Pool/Health Club:** *No*
Room telephones: *Yes*	**Conference Facilities:** *Up to 120*
TV in Rooms: *Yes*	**Price Guide:** *Single £58.50 Double £98.50*
Pets: *By arrangement*	**Location:** *Off A914 Glenrothes-Tay Bridge/Dundee, 1*
Children: *Yes*	*mile north of A91/A914 Melville roundabout.*

LOCH NESS LODGE HOTEL

Drumnadrochit, Inverness-shire IV3 6TJ
Tel: 01456 450342 Fax: 01456 450429 USA Toll Free Tel: 1-800-365-6537

Dating back to around 1740, this unusual hotel is synonomous with the famous Loch from which it takes its name. Once the home of a colonial tea planter, it stands in eight acres of delightful grounds. Situated 14 miles from Inverness, it is a favourite spot for tourists. The hotel offers elegant en suite bedrooms and fresh imaginatively prepared food. The best prime Aberdeen Angus beef, West Coast seafood from Mallaig and Kinlochbervie, local venison, wild mushrooms and fresh garden vegetables. The hotel is linked to the Visitor Centre with its unique exhibition which attracts people from around the world. A warm welcome, friendly staff, outstanding cuisine and first class service make a holiday at the Loch Ness Lodge Hotel a memorable experience.

Open: *Mar.-Nov.*
No. Rooms: *50 En Suite 50*
Room telephones: *Yes*
TV in Rooms: *Yes*
Pets: *No*   **Children:** *Yes*
Disabled: *Yes*

Swimming Pool/Health Club: *No*
Conference Facilities: *Up to 20*
Price Guide: *Single £50.00 Double £70.00-£100.00*
Location: *14 miles south of Inverness on Fort William Road.*

HETLAND HALL HOTEL

Carrutherstown, Dumfries DG1 4JX

Tel: 01387 840201 Fax: 01387 840211 USA Toll Free Tel: 1-800-365-6537

Hetland Hall is an elegant Georgian country mansion house, set in 45 acres of wooded parkland between Carlisle and Dumfries. Under the guidance of resident proprietors, David, Mary and Christopher Allen, Hetland has been carefully and sympathetically refurbished to a very high standard. The single, double, twin and family rooms are all en suite with bath or shower room. The public rooms look south over lawns to the Solway and beyond whilst spacious lounges are ideal to relax with a newspaper or to have discussions with a colleague or friends. There is a wide range of recreational activities on offer including an indoor heated swimming pool. The 'Copper Beech' restaurant enjoys a substantial local reputation with menus reflecting the chef's imaginative use of seasonal produce from the area. A warm welcome is assured and the service provided is efficient and friendly, whilst maintaining an atmosphere of enjoyable informality.

Open: *All year*	**Swimming Pool/Health Club:** *Yes*
No. Rooms: *27 En Suite 27*	**Conference Facilities:** *10-200*
Room telephones: *Yes*	**Price Guide:** *Single £59.00-78.00 Double £82.00-109.00*
TV in Rooms: *Yes*	**Location:** *Midway between Annan and Dumfries off A75.*
Pets: *Yes* **Children:** *Yes*	
Disabled: *Yes*	

DUNDONNELL HOTEL

Little Loch Broom, nr. Ullapool, Ross-shire IV23 2QR
Tel: 01854 633204 Fax: 01854 633366 USA Toll Free Tel: 1-800-365-6537

Sheltering beneath the towering An Teallach mountain range and enjoying superb views down Little Loch Broom, Dundonnell Hotel is one of the leading hotels in the northern Highlands. The Florence family continue to build upon their enviable reputation for award winning food, accommodation and hospitality. Bedrooms are furnished to a very high standard and the cuisine has earned the hotel an AA red rosette for food and a 74% rating. Although 'away from it all' which adds to its attraction, this is the only 3 star establishment in the Ullapool area. The staff display a very high standard of attentiveness but retain an informal manner which is friendly but efficient. The attractive and unusual coffered ceilinged dining room with views over the loch offers ever changing imaginative menus with a strong emphasis on the natural cooking of Scotland. Here in this wild and beautiful region visitors enjoy unusual standards of civilised comfort and it is an ideal location for exploring the North West of Scotland.

Open: *Feb.-Nov. & Xmas & New Year*
No. Rooms: *30 En Suite 30*
Room telephones: *Yes*
TV in Rooms: *Yes*
Pets: *Yes*   **Children:** *Yes*
Disabled: *Please enquire*

Swimming Pool/Health Club: *No*
Conference Facilities: *Up to 30*
Price Guide: *Single £40.00-£60.00 Double £60.00-£99.00*
Location: *On A832 on the shores of Little Loch Broom, just south of Ullapool.*

KINNAIRD

Kinnaird Estate, By Dunkeld, Perthshire PH8 0LB
Tel: 01796 482440 Fax: 01796 482289 USA Toll Free Tel: 1-800-365-6537

A member of the prestigious Relais & Chateaux Kinnaird is set on a bluff in the middle of its own 9000 acres overlooking the Tay River Valley. The building has been restored to its former glory by its owner Mrs Constance Ward. The gardens are immaculate and there is a feeling of well being when you drive up to the front of the house. Superb cuisine can be enjoyed in two exquisite dining rooms, one of which overlooks the river Tay. As one would expect the bedrooms have been individually decorated with fabrics and furnishings to complement the size of the rooms and the views. The large private bathrooms have been retained in the traditional style of the house. Public rooms are furnished almost entirely with fine and rare pieces of furniture, china and pictures. Kinnaird also offers a wide range of outdoor pursuits. Although a hotel Kinnaird has been described as a comfortable, beautiful but cosy home that happens to be a hotel. It upholds the finest traditions of hotel keeping. Member of the Scotch Beef Club.

Open: *All year except during Jan/Feb when only open Thurs.-Sun. inc.*	**Children:** *Over 12* **Disabled:** *Yes*
No. Rooms: *9 En Suite 9*	**Swimming Pool/Health Club:** *No*
Room telephones: *Yes*	**Conference Facilities:** *Small business meeting Director level*
TV in Rooms: *Yes*	**Price Guide:** *Double May-Oct.* **£220-£275,** *Suite* **£295.00**
Pets: *In kennels*	*Nov.-Apr.* **£225.00 (incl. Dinner)** *All Rooms*
	Location: *2 miles north of Dunkeld on A9 – take B898 turn off.*

STAKIS DUNKELD
Dunkeld, Perthshire PH8 0HX
Tel: 01350 727771 Fax: 01350 728924 USA Toll Free Tel: 1-800-365-6537

The hotel was built by the 7th Duke of Atholl in the last century as the perfect highland home just 12 miles north of Perth. It stands on the banks of the Tay, one of Scotland's finest salmon rivers and is set in 280 acres of beautiful grounds surrounded by the magnificent Perthshire countryside. All 85 bedrooms are individually furnished with bathrooms en suite. Each room is equipped with every modern convenience and there are a number that overlook the Tay itself. The restaurant creates several imaginative dishes skilfully prepared with the emphasis being on a modern Scottish cuisine flavour. The leisure and sporting facilities are unrivalled among country house hotels in Scotland offering salmon fishing, clay pigeon shooting, 4x4 off road driving and indoor swimming pool among a long list of activities for fitness and relaxation. The ever courteous General Manager Dick Beach and his trained staff will assist with every arrangement to make your visit a complete success.

Open: *All year*
No. Rooms: *85 En Suite 85*
Room telephones: *Yes*
TV in Rooms: *Yes*
Pets: *Yes* **Children:** *Yes*
Disabled: *Yes*

Swimming Pool/Health Club: *Yes*
Conference Facilities: *Up to 90 delegates*
Price Guide: *Double £116.00-£130.00.*
Location: *A9 12 miles north of Perth – through village of Dunkeld and turn left, through gateway.*

JOHNSTOUNBURN HOUSE HOTEL

Humbie, nr. Edinburgh, East Lothian EH36 5PL
Tel: 01875 833696 Fax: 01875 833626 USA Toll Free Tel: 1-800-365-6537

It has taken the best part of four centuries to create the unique setting of Johnstounburn House which is now a luxury hotel just 15 miles south of Edinburgh on the A68. Built in 1625 it is the perfect retreat surrounded by attractive gardens and enclosed by traditional walls and formal yew hedges. Host Ken Chernoff who has been here for many years displays a certain charisma and his distinctive personality makes one at ease and from the moment you arrive you feel 'at home'. Each of the 20 bedrooms in either the main house or in the original coach house are individually and attractively furnished with all modern facilities. The 18th century panelled dining room offers table d'hote dishes which are excellently complimented by a large wine list - mainly French and European. There are many golf courses to choose from including the famous Muirfield championship course at Gullane - clay pigeon shooting is available on the estate, as are off road driving, trout fishing, and a practice golf fairway. The house can also accommodate board or management meetings for up to 20 people and corporate business is welcome.

Open: *All year*	**Swimming Pool/Health Club:** *Leisure outdoor facilities*
No. Rooms: *20 En Suite 19*	**Conference Facilities:** *Up to 20 Boardroom*
Room telephones: *Yes*	**Price Guide:** *Single £110.00 Double £140.00*
TV in Rooms: *Yes*	**Location:** *15 miles south east of Edinburgh on A68. Turn off at Fala Village*
Pets: *Yes* **Children:** *Yes*	
Disabled: *Limited*	

THE ROXBURGHE HOTEL

Charlotte Square, Edinburgh EH2 4HG

Tel: 0131-225 3921 Fax: 0131-220 2518 USA Toll Free Tel: 1-800-365-6537

This distinguished hotel, with an international reputation, is situated in Charlotte Square, one of the most perfect examples of Adam architecture completed in the 19th century. The Roxburghe continues a long established tradition of discreet personal attention performed with quiet good humour. Its style is more reminiscent of a country house than a city hotel. Its period furniture and Adam fireplace echo a bygone era. The individual character of the hotel is reflected in the variety of bedrooms and their decor. The comfort of the guests is of the utmost importance. Enjoy a relaxed meal in the Consort restaurant where the menu includes Scottish and International dishes with an extensive choice. Only 5 minutes from Princes Street but also within easy reach of Gleneagles and St. Andrews, The Borders, The Clyde, The Trossachs and part of the highlands are close enough to visit in a single day and still return to The Roxburghe for dinner.

Open: *All year*
No. Rooms: *75 En Suite 75*
Room telephones: *Yes*
TV in Rooms: *Yes*
Pets: *On request*
Children: *Yes*

Disabled: *Limited*
Swimming Pool/Health Club: *No*
Conference Facilities: *Theatre/Banquet 250*
Price Guide: *Single £95.00-£99.00 Double £120.00-£135.00*
Location: *West End of George Street at Charlotte Square*

ALLT-NAN-ROS HOTEL

Onich, by Fort William, Inverness-shire PH33 6RY
Tel: 01855 821210 Fax: 01855 821462 USA Toll Free Tel: 1-800-365-6537

Allt-nan-Ros is Gaelic for "the burn of the roses" and the name derives from the enchanting cascading stream which passes through the gardens of the hotel and on into Loch Leven & Loch Linnhe. From an elevated site the hotel enjoys quite exceptional views across spectacular mountain scenery, and along the loch, beyond Appin and towards the Isle of Mull. This Victorian house, owned by the MacLeod family has been tastefully upgraded into its present form - en suite bedrooms with quality furnishings - some superior rooms with views over the loch. The lounge, foyer and dining room are richly furnished in traditional style, where fresh flowers abound. The cuisine is French with a strong west highland flavour. Accolades include a 4 crown highly commended rating from the STB, 2 AA red rosettes for food and recommended by Egon Ronay. Fort William is only 10 miles north of Onich and 5 miles from historic Glencoe and there is easy access to the Ardnamurchan Peninsula via the Corran ferry. There are also ferry crossings to Mull, Skye, Eigg, Rum, Muck or Canna - all this within easy reach from Allt-nan-Ros.

Open: *Closed Mid./Nov.-29th Dec.*	**Swimming Pool/Health Club:** *No*
No. Rooms: *20 En Suite 20*	**Conference Facilities:** *No*
Room telephones: *Yes*	**Price Guide:** *£50-£75 D., B. & B.*
TV in Rooms: *Yes*	**Location:** *On A82, 10 miles south of Fort William.*
Pets: *Yes* **Children:** *Yes*	
Disabled: *Unsuitable*	

CULDEARN HOUSE

Woodlands Terrace, Grantown-on-Spey, Moray PH26 3JU
Tel: 01479 872106 Fax: 01479 873641 USA Toll Free Tel: 1-800-365-6537

My book would not be complete without an entry from the Spey Valley and Culdearn House was the obvious choice. I have witnessed Alasdair and Isobel Little's progress over the years and they exemplify highland hospitality at its very best. The recipients of many accolades over the years Culdearn was awarded the accolade 'Best Small Hotel in Scotland' from the RAC in 1995 (yet another invitation to London). This Victorian house on the outskirts of the town has 9 en suite bedrooms beautifully furnished to a high standard. The menu changes daily and Isobel 'leaves no stone unturned' using fresh local produce in skilfully prepared dishes. There is a distinct Scottish atmosphere within the hotel and the enthusiasm and genuine welcome by Alasdair and Isobel make all the difference to your stay – you really feel 'at home'. Leisure activities abound and the Cairngorm mountains beckon in the distance.

Open: *Mar.-Oct.*
No. Rooms: *9 En Suite 9*
Room telephones: *No*
TV in Rooms: *Yes*
Pets: *No*
Children: *Over 10*

Disabled: *Unsuitable*
Swimming Pool/Health Club: *No*
Conference Facilities: *No*
Price Guide: *Single £55.00 (incl. dinner) Double £110.00 (incl. dinner).*
Location: *A95, south west entry to Grantown-on-Spey.*

CULLODEN HOUSE

Culloden, Inverness IV1 2NZ
Tel: 01463 790461 Fax: 01463 792181 USA Toll Free Fax: 1-800-373-7987

A new regime has been installed at Culloden House with Major Gillis (USA) heading up a very efficient team and co-owner Ed Cunningham applying his expertise gained from the 'trade' in the USA. This site has many historical and romantic associations with Bonnie Prince Charlie and the Battle of Culloden fought nearby. This is a magnificent building surrounded by fine lawns and acres of parkland which sets the hotel off to best advantage. The bedrooms are excellently appointed, spacious and furnished to a very high standard - several have 4 poster beds. The Adam dining room and public rooms are tastefully furnished and retain the ambience which fits in perfectly with the character of the house. Chef of note Michael Simpson presents menus which are a delightful blend of classical and Scottish country house cooking and offers a wide range of skillfully prepared dishes. For all round quality the only word to describe Culloden House is excellent. Member of The Scotch Beef Club.

Open: *All year*	**Disabled:** *Unsuitable*
No. Rooms: *25 En Suite 25*	**Swimming Pool/Health Club:** *No*
Room telephones: *Yes*	**Conference Facilities:** *Up to 45*
TV in Rooms: *Yes*	**Price Guide:** *Single £130.00 Double £185.00-£240.00.*
Pets: *By arrangement*	**Location:** *A96 3 miles south of Inverness. 5 miles from*
Children: *Over 10*	*Inverness Airport.*

DUNAIN PARK HOTEL

Dunain Park, Inverness IV3 6JN
Tel: 01463 230512 Fax: 01463 224532 USA Toll Free Tel: 1-800-365-6537

This very fine Georgian country house is set in 6 acres of secluded woodland just outside Inverness on the Fort William road. The 14 en suite bedrooms are extremely well furnished the suites being particularly elegant. There is also the coach-house in the grounds converted to two family suites, both with their own lounge. Public rooms are furnished with antiques, original oil paintings and have log fires. Owners Edward and Ann Nicoll pride themselves on their award winning restaurant where cuisine is Scottish but with a French influence. Two acres of walled garden supply herbs, soft fruit and vegetables. There is home-baking, home made jams and fresh local produce such as wild salmon, according to the season. Situated only a mile outside Inverness this is an ideal centre for touring the Highlands. STB 4 crown de luxe and member of The Scotch Beef Club.

Open: *All year*
No. Rooms: *12 En Suite bedrooms*
Room telephones: *Yes*
TV in Rooms: *Yes*
Pets: *Yes* **Children:** *Yes*
Disabled: *Yes*

Swimming Pool: *Use of pool is restricted to residents.*
Conference Facilities: *Small business meetings*
Price Guide: *Double £130.00-£158.00*
Location: *A82 Fort William road 1 mile west of Inverness*

KINGSMILLS HOTEL

Culcabock Road, Inverness IV2 3LP
Tel: 01463 237166 Fax: 01463 225208 USA Toll Free Tel: 1-800-365-6537

This popular Inverness hotel was built in 1785 and has been thoughtfully extended to create a blend of luxury and elegance. It is situated on the outskirts of the city next to Inverness golf course in 3 acres of well maintained gardens. The hotel offers luxury accommodation with purpose built family rooms/suites and a range of facilities that suit the holiday maker, family or business person. Apart from the beautifully appointed bedrooms there are six luxury villas that overlook the golf course. The leisure club includes, an indoor swimming pool, spa bath, sauna, steam room, mini-gym, hairdressing salon, solarium and the pitch/putt course. The Kingsmills restaurant is well known for its a la carte and table d'hote menus, prepared with the finest of Scottish ingredients. Light meals are also available for lunch and dinner in the conservatory and lounge areas, as well as a full 24 hour room service. There are numerous places/sites of historic interest to visit and the hotel is only a 20 minute drive from Inverness airport.

Open: *All year*	**Swimming Pool/Health Club:** *Yes*
No. Rooms: *84 En Suite 84*	**Conference Facilities:** *Yes – 3 venues for up to 60*
Room telephones: *Yes*	**Price Guide:** *Single £105.00-£130.00 Double £145.00-£175.00*
TV in Rooms: *Yes*	**Location:** *From A9 signposted Kingsmills/golf course. Turn*
Pets: *Yes* **Children:** *Yes*	*left immediately after the traffic lights past the golf*
Disabled: *Yes*	*course.*

STEVENSONS

LOCH NESS & GREAT GLEN CRUISE COMPANY

Muirtown Top Lock, Caledonian Canal, Canal Road, Inverness IV3 6NF
Tel: 01463 711913 Fax: 01463 711913 Ship Radio Tel: 0421 895492
USA Toll Free Tel: 1-800-365-6537

There can be no better way to enjoy the wonder of Scotland's spectacular scenery than a cruise on the Caledonian Canal and Loch Ness. "The Spirit of Loch Ness" offers the luxury of a few days spent in idleness away from the rush and bustle of modern day living. Robin Black has used all his expertise as a hotelier to encompass the gracious living of a top class hotel. There are 3 twin-berth and 1 double berth cabins which can accommodate 8 guests in comfort and each cabin is fully en suite - meals are taken in the raised dining area between the saloon and well equipped galley and there is a very high standard of cuisine. In the saloon guests can sit and read, play cards or board games or just enjoy the disappearing pleasure of conversation. You will find yourself being pampered by your friendly host and staff as you cruise gently through the famous lochs - stopping at places of interest and catching the odd sight of Eagle or Osprey - or even "Nessie" herself… The cruise takes you from Inverness to Fort William - between the North Sea and the Atlantic Ocean on a 3 or 6 night excursion.

Open: *Apr.-Oct. Charter all year round*	**Disabled:** *Unsuitable*
No. Cabins: *4 En Suite 4*	**Swimming Pool/Health Club:** *No*
Room telephones: *No*	**Conference Facilities:** *Limited - Director level only*
TV in Rooms: *Lounge only*	**Price Guide:** *3 night cruise £400 6 night cruise £780*
Pets: *No*	**Location:** *Old A9 on Caledonian Canal.*
Children: *Over 16*	

ARDSHEAL HOUSE

Kentallen of Appin, Argyll PA38 4BX
Tel: 01631 740227 Fax: 01631 740342 USA Toll Free Tel: 1-800-365-6537

This well appointed building which has strong 'associations' with the Jacobite Rebellion stands in 900 acres of hills, woods, garden and shore front. It is both imposing and gracious and has commanding views over Loch Linnhe. Ardsheal has a very good reputation for food here and abroad and is blessed with local salmon, prawns, oysters and trout. An excellent wine list and wide choice of malt whiskies add to the enjoyment of the meal. There are 13 comfortable bedrooms all with private bathrooms of which 11 are en suite and individually furnished with family antiques. Two comfortable sitting rooms lead off from the oak panelled staircase where one can relax and enjoy the sun setting over the loch. In addition to the billiards room other forms of relaxation include the extensive gardens and tennis. Other leisure pursuits can be arranged. Ardsheal House is an ideal base for exploring the Highlands making use of day trips.

Open: *Closed 31.1.97 - 27.3.97*	**Swimming Pool/Health Club:** *No*
No. Rooms: *13 En Suite 11*	**Conference Facilities:** *Up to 25*
Room telephones: *Yes*	**Price Guide:** *Single £85.00-£130.00 Double £65.00-£90.00*
TV in Rooms: *No*	*Special winter rates for D.B.&B.*
Pets: *Yes* **Children:** *Yes*	**Location:** *On A828, 4 miles south of Ballachulish Bridge.*
Disabled: *Unsuitable*	

ARDANAISEIG HOTEL
Kilchrenan, by Taynuilt, Argyll PA35 1HE
Tel: 01866 833333 Fax: 01866 833222 USA Toll Free Tel: 1-800-365-6537

Recently purchased by Professor Benjamin Gray, Ardanaiseig stands in a truly idyllic setting on Loch Awe looking towards Ben Cruachan and surrounded by shrub and woodland gardens renowned for many rare species. Benjamin Gray has now enlisted the services of hotelier Robert Francis from London as General Manager and Janet Reid as his assistant - together they make a formidable team which offers the stability that Ardansiseig deserves. The bedrooms are quite luxurious, individually furnished with views over the loch or garden - the public rooms are spacious with log fires, comfortable chairs and are furnished with antique furniture. The restaurant is noted for its imaginative use of fresh produce for which the West of Scotland is famous. Chef Dale Thornber focuses his cuisine on local ingredients, carefully prepared and describes his food as traditional but with an exotic combination. This hotel offers tranquility, privacy, every comfort and a real feeling of well being. I have known this hotel for many years and have the "feel good factor" about Benjamin Gray and his staff at Ardanaiseig.

Open: *Feb. 14 - Jan. 2nd*	**Disabled:** *Unsuitable*
No. Rooms: *14 En Suite 14*	**Swimming Pool/Health Club:** *No*
Room telephones: *Yes*	**Conference Facilities:** *Yes*
TV in Rooms: *Yes*	**Price Guide:** *Single £72.00-£116.00 Double £84,00-£172.00*
Pets: *Yes*	**Location:** *Near Oban on West Coast. A85 to Taynuilt then B845.*
Children: *Over 8*	*At Kilchrenan take road signposted for hotel - 3 miles.*

BALLATHIE HOUSE

Kinclaven, By Stanley, Perthshire, PH1 4QN
Tel: 01250 883268 Fax: 01250 883396 USA Toll Free Tel: 1-800-365-6537

A previous winner of the MACALLAN award for Country House Hotel of the year, Ballathie is a magnificent building sitting in its own estate on the banks of the River Tay. The main driveway to the hotel is an experience in itself and exudes opulence, with lawns stretching down to the Tay. Entering the hotel, one feels immediately at ease from a very friendly staff under the supervision of Chris Longden. There are well proportioned public rooms and very comfortable bedrooms each with its own character and style. Ballathie is a member of the Scotch Beef Club as indicated by the Black Bull below the main picture. This reflects that only the best of produce is used in an ever changing menu and the food is skilfully prepared and presented to a high standard. I can assure you of a very warm welcome at Ballathie and a strong feeling that, when you leave, you will return.

Open: *All year*
No. Rooms: *27 En Suite 27*
Room telephones: *Yes*
TV in Rooms: *Yes*
Pets: *Yes* **Children:** *Yes*
Disabled: *Yes*

Swimming Pool/Health Club: *No*
Conference Facilities: *Small business meetings*
Price Guide: *Single £62.50-£82.50 Double £115,00-£180.00*
2 Day breaks from £69.00 P.P.P.N.
Location: *Off A9, 2 miles North of Perth through Stanley/or off A93 at Beech hedge and signs.*

STEVENSONS

THE GREEN HOTEL

2 The Muirs, Kinross KY13 7AS
Tel: 01577 863467 Fax: 01577 863180 USA Toll Free Tel: 1-800-365-6537

Although just a short drive from Edinburgh or Perth you immediately feel that you are in the countryside. The Green Hotel is situated near Loch leven which has close historic ties with Mary Queen of Scots and is a popular area for the fishing fraternity. Formerly a coaching inn there is a wide range of leisure activities including golf (2 courses) curling rink, putting green, all weather tennis courts, croquet, squash, heated pool, sauna, fitness area and games room. The spacious bedrooms are furnished and decorated to a high standard – some with 4 posters. There is an attractive cocktail bar and large dining area serving the very best of Scottish and International cuisine. Conference facilities prove very popular at this hotel yet do not interfere with the enjoyment of the holiday maker or that weekend away from it all. Also popular at the hotel is 'the shop at the Green'.

Open: *All year*
No. Rooms: *47 En Suite 47*
Room telephones: *Yes*
TV in Rooms: *Yes*
Pets: *Yes* **Children:** *Yes*
Disabled: *Yes*

Swimming Pool/Health Club: *Yes*
Conference Facilities: *Up to 100*
Price Guide: *Single £70.00-£90.00 Double £100.00-£135.00*
Location: *M90 between Edinburgh and Perth – turn off at Junction 6 – Kinross signpost.*

LESLIE CASTLE

Leslie, by Insch, Aberdeenshire AB52 6NX
Tel: 01464 820869 Fax: 01464 821076 USA Toll Free Tel: 1-800-365-6537

Leslie Castle in Aberdeenshire is situated at the west end of the Bennachie range 30 miles north west of Aberdeen. The original seat of the Clan Leslie, the castle is the third fortified building on the site since 1070. In 1979 the present owners and hosts David and Leslie Leslie, (Baron and Baroness) acquired the decaying roofless ruin and after 10 years the castle has been transformed into a fairy tale 17th century fortified house. The baronial hall with timber beamed ceiling, large fireplace and stone flagged floor creates a fitting atmosphere to enjoy a very high standard of Scottish and International cuisine prepared personally by the Baroness. The 4 bedroom accommodation includes 2 four poster bedrooms, one double bedroom and one twin bedroom all en suite, very spacious and with every facility. Bedrooms are suitable for family use. This is a castle in the true sense of the word and an ideal base for touring the Grampian area.

Open: *All year*
No. Rooms: *4 En Suite 4*
Room telephones: *Yes*
TV in Rooms: *Yes*
Pets: *No* **Children:** *Yes*
Disabled: *Unsuitable*

Swimming Pool/Health Club: *No*
Conference Facilities: *Small business meetings up to 12*
Price Guide: *Single £87.00-£95.00 Double £124.00-£140.00*
Location: *Two miles west of the B992 Auchleven/Leslie crossroads.*

INVER LODGE HOTEL

Lochinver, Sutherland IV27 4LU

Tel: 01571 844496 Fax: 01571 844395 USA Toll Free Tel: 1-800-365-6537

This superb and modern hotel was opened in April 1988. It stands in this wild region of Scotland in an elevated position which has breathtaking, panoramic views across Loch Inver Bay to the Hebrides. From the moment you enter the reception area you feel comfortable and no expense has been spared to extend every comfort for the visitor. Public rooms, bedrooms and the dining room are all spacious and furnished to a very high standard. The bedrooms are luxurious with fine furnishings and wide beds to the degree of opulence. Wide corridors and staircase lead to the dining room which overlooks the bay through large glass windows. Sunsets are spectacular and the cuisine could be described as the same. The steak and lamb I can recommend personally but there is an ever changing menu with a variety of choices. The service at Inver Lodge is second to none and Nicholas Gorton, General Manager, has to be complemented on his attention to every detail but always making you 'feel at home'.

Open: *Mid April-end Oct.*
No. Rooms: *20 En Suite 20*
Room telephones: *Yes*
TV in Rooms: *Yes*
Pets: *Yes* **Children:** *Yes*
Disabled: *Unsuitable*

Swimming Pool/Health Club: *No*
Conference Facilities: *No*
Price Guide: *Single £80.00 Double £120.00*
Location: *Through village on A835 and turn left after village hall.*

MELFORT PIER & HARBOUR

Kilmelford, by Oban, Argyll PA34 4XD
Tel: 01852 200333 Fax: 01852 200329 USA Toll Free Tel: 1-800-365-6537

"An escape for all seasons" is how you can describe Melfort Pier & Harbour located on Loch Melfort - one of the most beautiful areas of Scotland. Although not a hotel there are 10 self catering harbour houses which offer the ultimate in luxury living and command a 5 crown de luxe rating from the STB. The views are spectacular. There is a choice of 2 or 3 bedroomed houses which are finished to the highest of standards, providing freedom, flexibility, privacy and service. Sensible and thoughtful design make the harbour houses blend with the environment and each property is to a Scandanavian design with all "home from home" comforts. Each house is different in layout and vary in size to sleep 2-6 persons. In the 2 and 3 bedroomed houses each bedroom has its own en suite facility which is opulence indeed. Leisure activities abound including water sports and the area is second to none for wildlife and walking. There are panoramic views to Jura, Mull & Colonsay and visits to National Trust properties. This is indeed an extremely comfortable base to relax and unwind and choose the things you want to do when you want to do them.

Open: *All year*	**Swimming Pool/Health Club:** *Sauna & Spa bath in each house*
No. Houses: *10 En Suite 10+*	**Conference Facilities:** *Up to 12 - Director level*
Room telephones: *Yes*	**Price Guide:** *From £90.00-£160.00 per house / per night*
TV in Rooms: *Yes/Satellite TV*	*Minimum stay - 2 nights*
Pets: *2 per House* **Children:** *Yes*	**Location:** *A816-17 miles north of Lochgilphead or A816-15 miles*
Disabled: *Yes*	*south of Oban. Well signposted-1½ miles from A816.*

CRAIGDARROCH HOUSE HOTEL

Foyers, Loch Ness Side, Inverness-Shire IV1 2XU
Tel: 01456 486400 Fax: 01456 486444 USA Toll Free Tel: 1-800-365-6537

Craigdarroch Hotel commands an elevated position high above Loch Ness on the south side of the loch and enjoys quite splendid panoramic views. Although the Munro family have been in the area for some time the hotel was only opened in 1994. It has already been awarded 4 crown highly commended by the STB. I can assure you of a warm welcome from hosts Kate & David Munro who operate a first class establishment. The spacious drawing room leads to a magnificent conservatory where you can sit and enjoy the views and to the rear is the cosy lounge bar. Bedrooms offer all the essentials in guest care - some with 4 posters and most have views over the loch. Son Andrew is the chef of some repute with varied menus to delight all tastes. There are many leisure activities to pursue in this area as would be expected but my main impression of an evening was the friendliness created by our hosts and their staff. There is also many a tale of "Nessie" to tell after dinner when you are enjoying your brandy & coffee. Member of The Scotch Beef Club. Well recommended.

Open: *Feb.-Dec. (Inclusive)*
No. Rooms: *12 En Suite 12*
Room telephones: *Yes*
TV in Rooms: *Yes*
Pets: *Yes* **Children:** *Yes*
Disabled: *Yes*

Swimming Pool/Health Club: *No*
Conference Facilities: *Up to 20*
Price Guide: *Single £60.00 Double £120.00*
Location: *20 minutes from Inverness on the Southern Shore of Loch Ness. B862 sign posted Dores then B852 to Foyers. From Fort Augustus B862 to just beyond White Bridge B852 to Foyers. Hotel sign posted.*

BURTS HOTEL

Market Square, Melrose, Roxburghshire TD6 9PN
Tel: 01896 822285 Fax: 01896 822870 USA Toll Free Tel: 1-800-365-6537

Built in 1722 Burts Hotel nestles in the shadow of the Eildon Hills in the very heart of the Scottish Borders. Melrose and the borders of Scotland are enriched with stories of Scotland's past and there are a number of abbeys, stately homes and gardens to visit. The hotel has been owned by the Henderson family for 24 years and they have built up an enviable reputation in the area. Every modern comfort is available and the 21 en suite bedrooms are exceptional. The refurbished restaurant is elegance itself offering cooking at its best and where the emphasis is on the abundance of local game and fresh fish. There is a very popular lounge bar serving delicious food as recommended by Egon Ronay Good Food Guide. There are also over 60 malt whiskies to choose from. Golf courses are within easy reach and salmon and trout fishing can be arranged on the famous River Tweed. The ideal base for touring the borders of Scotland. STB 4 crown highly commended, AA 3 star and 2 food rosettes. Member of The Scotch Beef Club.

Open: *All year except 24-26th Dec.*
No. Rooms: *21 En Suite 21*
Room telephones: *Yes*
TV in Rooms: *Yes*
Pets: *Yes* **Children:** *Yes*
Disabled: *Limited*

Swimming Pool/Health Club: *No*
Conference Facilities: *Up to 36*
Price Guide: *Single £48.00-£52.00 Double £78.00-£84.00*
Location: *A6091, 2 miles from A68, 38 miles south of Edinburgh.*

DUNGALLAN HOUSE HOTEL

Gallanach Road, Oban, Argyll PA34 4PD
Tel: 01631 563799 Fax: 01631 566711 USA Toll Free Tel: 1-800-365-6537

Dungallan House, built in 1870 by the Campbell family, stands on an elevated position commanding spectacular views over Oban Bay to the islands of Mull and Lismore. George and Janice Stewart, who arrived here last year after 13 years at Arisaig Hotel, are firmly resolved to maintain a high standard of all round hospitality using their expertise from Arisaig. The house has undergone a major programme of upgrading which has been carried out to retain the character and elegance of the building. The cuisine is quite outstanding with Janice using all her experience she gained at Arisaig. The views overlooking the bay from the dining room add to the enjoyment of the meal. Bedrooms are comfortable and well equipped. Although only 15 minutes walk to the centre of Oban the hotel is quite isolated in 5 acres of well kept grounds and steeped craggy tree lined cliffs which makes you feel that you are in the country. Oban is the main ferry terminal to Mull and the outer Isles. Member of The Scotch Beef Club.

Open: *All year except part Feb. and Nov.*	**Swimming Pool/Health Club:** *No*
No. Rooms: *13 En Suite 11*	**Conference Facilities:** *Up to 20 off season*
Room telephones: *No*	**Price Guide:** *Single £40.00 Double £80.00*
TV in Rooms: *Yes*	**Location:** *From Argyll Square in Oban follow signs for*
Pets: *Dogs* **Children:** *Yes*	*Gallanch – half mile.*
Disabled: *Yes*	

NEWMILN COUNTRY HOUSE HOTEL

By Scone Palace, Guildtown, Perth PH2 6AE
Tel: 01738 552364 Fax: 01738 553505 USA Toll Free Tel: 1-800-365-6537

This outstanding well appointed Edwardian house stands within 7oo acres of woodland estate where pheasant, duck and trap shooting are available to guests. James and Elaine McFarlane have transformed the main house into a luxury country house with 7 bedrooms - spacious, tastefully decorated and furnished. The "Gone with the Wind" staircase, roaring log fires, intricate wood panelling and beautifully proportioned public rooms offers guests a style of hospitality which is rich but cosy. Chef J. Paul Burns has recently earned the AA accolade of 3 red rosettes which is quite an outstanding achievement - not too many establishments can boast such an award. There is a varied set menu each evening with interesting and imaginatively prepared dishes and with quality that is beyond reproach. The dining room is an experience in itself with polished mahogany tables, excellent food and friendly service with a quality of informality but attentiveness. Only a short distance from Perth, Newmiln, which is little known at the moment, offers a relaxing and memorable stay to which you will return.

Open: *All year (closed Xmas/Box. Day)*
No. Rooms: *4 En Suite, 3 Private*
Room telephones: *Yes*
TV in Rooms: *Yes*
Pets: *By arrange.* **Children:** *Over 12*
Disabled: *Yes*

Swimming Pool/Health Club: *No*
Conference Facilities: *Director level only*
Price Guide: *Single from £90.00 (inc. Dinner) Double from £160.00 (inc. Dinner)*
Location: *A93 4 miles north of Perth on Blairgowrie Road. Follow signs for Scone Palace-3½ miles after Scone Palace tree lined avenue signposted on left.*

POLMAILY HOUSE HOTEL
Drumnadrochit, Loch Ness, Inverness-Shire IV3 6XT
Tel: 01456 450343 Fax: 01456 450813 USA Toll Free Tel: 1-800-365-6537

Resident proprietors John & Sonia Whittington-Davis have transformed this country house hotel to one of the best establishments in the area. There is a distinctive character and atmosphere which is only possible in a privately owned, well run establishment where your hosts are committed to the highest standards. The grounds are spacious with sweeping lawns and recently a swimming pool has been built on the grounds next to the hotel. Bedrooms are individually decorated, tastefully furnished and have en suite facilities. There is the one glorious bedroom with a 4 poster for that special occasion. The cuisine is excellent and under the personal supervision of your host using an abundance of quality ingredients. There is a great deal of emphasis on the family at Polmaily and special facilities exist for children which are planned not to intrude on the privacy of other guests. Family fun includes pets & ponies, indoor heated swimming pool, Trout pond with boat, tree house, bikes, tennis court, croquet lawn, adventure playground and toddler area. Only 25 minutes from Inverness the area abounds with places of historic interest to visit-there are many leisure activities to enjoy including hill walking, riding, fishing & stalking. Guests arriving at Inverness by air or rail will be met by transport from the hotel.

Open: *All year*	**Swimming Pool/Health Club:** *Yes*
No. Rooms: *11 En Suite 11*	**Conference Facilities:** *10-20*
Room telephones: *Yes*	**Price Guide:** *£36.00 (Low Season) £62.00 (High Season)*
TV in Rooms: *Yes*	*B.&B. P.P.P.N. (Excludes Xmas & New Year)*
Pets: *Yes* **Children:** *Yes*	**Location:** *A831 from Drumnadrochit to Glen Affric*
Disabled: *Yes*	

EDDRACHILLES HOTEL

Badcall Bay, Scourie, Sutherland IV27 4TH
Tel: 01971 502080 Fax: 01971 502477 USA Toll Free Tel: 1-800-365-6537

This hotel is superbly situated on Badcall Bay with magnificent views. Set in 300 acres this building was a former manse and has been completely refurbished providing every comfort. This is a mecca for wildlife enthusiasts with native otters, seals, roe and red deer. Handa Island nearby is a bird sanctuary and there are many small islands in the bay that can be visited by boat. The 11 en suite bedrooms are comfortably furnished, some with views over the bay. The home cooking is a delight – I can vouch for the steaks myself served in the dining room with its exposed stone walls and original flagstone floor. A feature of the hotel is the sun porch which is tastefully furnished and where one can relax after dinner with coffee and liqueur. Owners Mr & Mrs Alasdair Wood, are always on hand to assist you during your stay and assure you of a memorable visit to the north west of Scotland.

Open: *March-October*
No. Rooms: *11 En Suite 11*
Room telephones: *Yes*
TV in Rooms: *Yes*
Pets: *No*   **Children:** *Over 3*
Disabled: *Unsuitable*

Swimming Pool/Health Club: *No*
Conference Facilities: *No*
Price Guide: *Single £40.00-£45.00 Double £65.00-£75.00*
Location: *Off A834 2 miles south of Scourie*

SKEABOST HOUSE HOTEL

Skeabost Bridge, Isle of Skye, Inverness-shire IV51 9NP
Tel: 01470 532202 Fax: 01470 532454 USA Toll Free Tel: 1-800-365-6537

Skeabost House Hotel on Skye is a luxurious establishment rich with contrasts. Set amidst beautifully landscaped gardens it overlooks Loch Snizort and is a picture of tranquillity. Dating back to 1870 the Scots pine panelling is a feature. There has been constant upgrading since the McNab/Stuart family bought the hotel in 1969 and additions have included the very popular conservatory which blends in with the building. The 'Black Bull logo' below the main picture signifies membership of the Scotch Beef Club – quality in itself. Chef Angus McNab uses only the best beef available but 'rings the changes' showing considerable flair and skill. The 26 en-suite bedrooms are furnished and decorated to a high standard. In 1984 a 9 hole golf course was built and other activities include fishing, walking and climbing. Niall McNab is always on hand to welcome guests and staff look after your every wish and endeavour to make your stay a memorable one. Free Golf and Free Salmon Fishing for 5 day stay or more.

Open: *April-October*	**Swimming Pool/Health Club:** *No*
No. Rooms: *26 En Suite 26*	**Conference Facilities:** *Up to 35*
Room telephones: *Yes*	**Price Guide:** *Single £46.00-£65.00 Double £80.00-£110.00*
TV in Rooms: *Yes*	*5 day terms D.B.B. from £345-£385*
Pets: *Yes* **Children:** *Yes*	**Location:** *4 miles north of Portree on Dunvegan road.*
Disabled: *Unsuitable*	

THE OLD MANOR HOTEL

Lundin Links, Near St. Andrews, Fife KY8 6AJ
Tel: 01333 320368 Fax: 01333 320911 USA Toll Free Tel: 1-800-365-6537

This extremely well positioned country house is near to the home of golf at St. Andrews. It commands extensive views over Largo Bay, Lundin Links and Leven Open qualifying golf courses. Only 45 minutes from Edinburgh and a short drive from St. Andrews it is well positioned for a number of leisure activities. Renowned for its all round hospitality The Old Manor Hotel prides itself on its reputation for food (AA rosette) and a very high standard of accommodation. The public rooms are comfortably furnished and spacious to allow for plenty of 'elbow room' which enjoy delightful sea views. Under the personal supervision of the Clark family there is no lack of attention to detail and the staff show every consideration which adds to the enjoyment of your stay.

Open: *All year*	**Swimming Pool/Health Club:** *No*
No. Rooms: *25 En Suite 25*	**Conference Facilities:** *Up to 100*
Room telephones: *Yes*	**Price Guide:** *Single £60.00-£65.00 Double £95.00-£105.00*
TV in Rooms: *Yes*	**Location:** *On A915 Kirkcaldy–St. Andrews, 1 mile east of*
Pets: *Yes* **Children:** *Yes*	*Leven, on right overlooking Largo Bay.*
Disabled: *Limited*	

PARK LODGE HOTEL

32 Park Terrace, Stirling FK8 2JS
Tel: 01786 474862 Fax: 01786 449748 USA Toll Free Tel: 1-800-365-6537

This is a fine Georgian mansion with walled garden situated in a delightful part of the town overlooking Stirling Castle. There are also fine views of the Campsie Fell hills and beyond. The furnishings are luxurious and reflect an era of gracious elegance. The bedrooms (some with 4 poster) are a delight – all en suite and again in the mould of a past era. The chef and owner Georges Marquetty holds court at The Heritage Restaurant which provides the best of food imaginatively prepared only using the very best of local produce. The lobster cocktail as a starter is a real treat in itself. There is a well stocked cocktail bar with a wide range of malt whiskies – tempting in itself after a splendid meal. There is so much of Scotland's heritage here in Stirling to see and visit. The film 'Braveheart' highlighted the story of Sir William Wallace. Only 15 minutes walk to the centre of the town.

Open: *All year*
No. Rooms: *10 En Suite 10*
Room telephones: *Yes*
TV in Rooms: *Yes*
Pets: *Yes* **Children:** *Yes*
Disabled: *Yes*

Swimming Pool/Health Club: *No*
Conference Facilities: *Up to 50, functions up to 150*
Price Guide: *Single from £50.00 Double from £75.00*

MANSFIELD HOUSE HOTEL

Scotsburn Road, Tain, Ross-Shire IV19 1PR
Tel: 01862 892052 Fax: 01862 892260 USA Toll Free Tel: 1-800-365-6537

This late Victorian Mansion house built in 1905 has been upgraded over the past 2 years to a luxury country house hotel. Resident proprietors, the Lauritsen family, now boast a 4 Crown Highly Commended rating from the STB. The bedrooms in the main house have been refurbished to their former glory all with en suite facilities. Features include plaster cornices and high ceilings. The master bedroom, the Haakon room, is named after the late King of Norway, who stayed in the house during the war. Its large bathroom is equipped with both a shower and jacuzzi. The modern wing is in keeping with the surroundings and has 10 well equipped bedrooms. The food combines international cooking and traditional Scottish fayre using the very best of local produce. The 'tear shaped' grounds are magnificent with sweeping lawns down to the entrance. There are excellent golfing facilities in the area with 8 courses to be found within a 25 mile radius including Royal Dornoch. Shooting and angling are other favourites. Tain is also the 'home' of the famous world renowned Glenmorangie malt whisky.

Open: *All year*	**Swimming Pool/Health Club:** *No*
No. Rooms: *17 En Suite 17*	**Conference Facilities:** *Up to 25*
Room telephones: *Yes*	**Price Guide:** *Single £45.00 - £55.00 Double £75.00 - £90.00*
TV in Rooms: *Yes*	**Location:** *From South - 2nd turning on right from A9*
Pets: *By arrange.* **Children:** *Yes*	*(Tain Bypass). Turn left then right into*
Disabled: *Unsuitable*	*Scotsburn Road. Hotel 200 metres on left.*

STONEFIELD CASTLE HOTEL

Tarbert, Loch Fyne, Argyll PA29 6YJ
Tel: 01880 820836 Fax: 01880 820929 USA Toll Free Tel: 1-800-365-6537

Stonefield Castle is set in 60 acres of woodland gardens that contain some of the finest Himalayan Rhododendrons and other exotic shrubs. The castle itself is a superb example of Scottish Baronial architecture built in 1837 and originally home to the Campbell family. It has retained much of the original furnishings, wood panelling, ornate ceilings and marble fireplaces alongside family portraits. Relax in the two spacious lounges or sample a pre-dinner drink in the panelled cocktail bar. Browse at your leisure and enjoy the spectacular views across Loch Fyne. Experience the very best of Scottish cuisine including shellfish, seasonal game and the famous Loch Fyne kipper. The food is complemented by a wine cellar of international repute. Recreational activities include golf, horse riding, sea and loch fishing. There is also a heated outdoor swimming pool.

Open: *All year*
No. Rooms: *33 En Suite 33*
Room telephones: *Yes*
TV in Rooms: *Yes*
Pets: *Yes*   **Children:** *Yes*
Disabled: *Yes*

Swimming Pool/Health Club: *Yes (outdoor)*
Conference Facilities: *Yes*
Price Guide: *Single £45.00-£75.00 P.P.P.N. Dinner, bed and breakfast*
Location: *From Lochgilphead take Tarbert Road South for 10 miles.*

MALIN COURT HOTEL

Turnberry, Ayrshire KA26 9PB

Tel: 01655 331457 Fax: 01655 331072 USA Toll Free Tel: 1-800-365-6537

Malin Court offers a perfect blend of informality, congeniality and the warmest of Scottish welcomes - all 17 bedrooms are en suite and provide every modern facility and have exquisite views overlooking either Turnberry's championship golf course or the mystical Isle of Arran and the Firth of Clyde. The Carrick Restaurant serves good quality food carefully prepared and using the best of local produce. Menus are complimented by a comprehensive wine list. Conference and banqueting facilities comprise of 4 splendid suites for up to 200 delegates and arrangements can be made for any special occasion. This is a very picturesque part of the Ayrshire coast with Culzean Castle nearby and in addition to golf the hotel can arrange shooting, horse riding, fishing and sailing. Although Turnberry is known for its golf course there is much to do and see in Ayrshire and Malin Court offers the ideal base for touring not only Ayrshire but the South West of Scotland.

Open: *All year*
No. Rooms: *17 En Suite 17*
Room telephones: *Yes*
TV in Rooms: *Yes*
Pets: *By arrange.* **Children:** *Yes*
Disabled: *Yes*

Swimming Pool/Health Club: *No*
Conference Facilities: *Up to 200*
Price Guide: *Single £72-£82.00 Double £52-£62.00 P.P.P.N.*
Location: *A719 Ayr-Girvan, South of Maidens.*

STEVENSONS

SCOTLAND'S GOOD HOTEL BOOK

1997

Feedback: **Alan Stevenson Publications**
4/3 Boat Green
Canonmills
Edinburgh   **Tel: 0131 556 2200**
EH3 5II   **Fax: 0131 557 6324**

Hotel: .... Length of Stay: ....

Hotel: .... Length of Stay: ....

Hotel: .... Length of Stay: ....

Hotel: .... Length of Stay: ....

Hotel: .... Length of Stay: ....

Comments ....

....

....

Any favourites not already included which you would like to recommend:

....

....

Your Name: ....

Address: ....

....

STEVENSONS

SCOTLAND'S GOOD HOTEL BOOK

1997

Order Form: Alan Stevenson Publications
4/3 Boat Green
Canonmills
Edinburgh   Tel: 0131 556 2200
EH3 5II   Fax: 0131 557 6324

Date: .... Please mail .... Copies of
Stevensons, Scotland's Good Hotel Book, 1997.

Your Name: ....

Address: ....

.... Postcode: ....

Retail Price	1 Book	2-5 Books	6-10 Books	11-20 Books
United Kingdom	£4.95	£4.50 each	£4.00 each	£3.50 each
USA only	$15.00	$13.00 each	$10.00 each	$8.00 each
Canada only	$20.00	$16.00 each	$12.00 each	$10.00 each
Europe	£7.50	£6.00 each	£5.00 each	£4.00 each
Outside Europe	£7.50	£6.00 each	£5.00 each	£4.00 each

Post & Packaging	1 Book	2-5 Books	6-10 Books	11-20 Books
United Kingdom	£0.55	£2.50	£4.00	£7.00
USA/Canada	$3.00	$5.00	$9.00	$16.00
Europe	£2.00	£3.50	£6.00	£10.00
Outside Europe	£3.00	£4.00	£6.50	£11.00

Payment in Pounds Sterling is preferred but payments can be accepted in American or Canadian Dollars, payable to Alan Stevenson Publications.

No. of Copies: ...... at £/$ .... each. Total £/$ ....

Post & Packaging   Total £/$ ....

I enclose a Cheque/Eurocheque for   Total £/$ ....
Please allow 28 days for delivery outwith the United Kingdom

Hotels listed alphabetically by name

See contents page for list of Trade Advertisers.

I N D E X